FROM ODDS AND ENDS TO
MAKIN
MODELS

DRAGON'S WORLD

CHILDREN'S BOOKS

This book is intended to help you make all sorts of models at almost no cost. Cartons and cylinders and containers are thrown away every day and many of these can be recycled to make fun models for display or toy models to play with. When you work with this book you should look closely at the diagrams and illustrations. You can copy them if you like, but they are really intended to help as you develop simple skills in making models.

You will need a place to work, felt-tips, scissors, glue strong enough to stick card and all sorts of saved scrap. You can find extra picture referenc[e] in books if you need to get information which yo[u] do not already have, but this is part of the fun[.]

You can start at the beginning of the book. It i[s] planned to lead a beginner stage by stage, but [if] you are confident you can start at any page. Places which must be folded in the models are printed as dotted lines. Places where you shoul[d] glue are also indicated. The suggestions are no[t] rules. They are there to guide and help you. Hav[e] fun MAKING MODELS.

Dragon's World Ltd
Limpsfield
Surrey RH8 ODY
Great Britain

First published by Dragon's World Ltd, 1995

Design: Michael Grater
In-house Design: Mel Raymond
Editor: Kyla Barber
Art Director: John Strange
Editorial Director: Pippa Rubinstein

The catalogue record for this book is available from the British Library

ISBN 1 85028 379 6

Printed in Italy

Contents

4   Standing Figures

6   Standing Animals

8   Homes

9   Surprise Street

10 Boats

12 Pit Stop

13 Space Shuttle

14 Dressed Figures

16 Cylinder Figures

17 Seated Figures

18 Mounted Figures

19 Cylinder Horses

20 Sloping Roofs

22 Chimneys, Doll's House and Shops

24 Sailing Ships

25 Mayflower

26 Container Ships

27 Roll-on Roll-off Ferry

28 Wheels – Chariot Racer

29 Pioneering Waggon

30 Tip-up Trucks

31 Tankers and Articulated Trucks

32 Going On

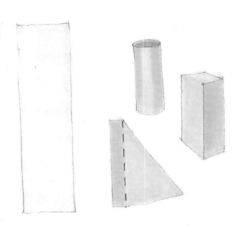

1

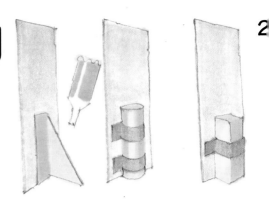

2

Standing Figures

The first stage in model making is to make things stand up.

A piece of card cut from one of your cartons will stand if you make a support at the back. The support can be a simple card bracket, a cylinder or a small box glued or taped to the card as shown in pictures 1 and 2.

When you can make the card stand you can begin to shape it, but in all model making it helps if the shapes are kept as simple as possible. A pattern cut in paper will give a simple shape for a figure, see 3 and 4.

Another pattern can be made for simple arms which you can stick at the back of the figure, see 5 and 6.

Try cutting some figures and decorating them with felt-tips. This is best done before you put the supporting fixture on the back.

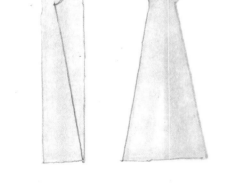

3

4

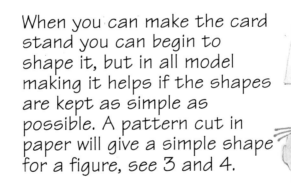

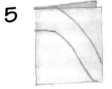

5

6

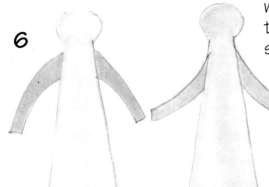

Once you can make a simple standing figure you can make them in all sorts of different costumes. You can use picture references, perhaps slightly varying the outline shape — figures from history or ones of special interest today.

On later pages you will see how the models can be developed, but at this stage you can create as many exciting and colourful figures as you like. It can be fun.

Standing Animals

It is as easy to make animal models as it is to make figures, but you must always aim for simplicity and must remember that you are model making — not drawing, and that you want your models to stand. You would have no trouble supporting a bulky elephant shape, but something like a giraffe with very thin legs would be more difficult. It would also be more of a problem to cut out.

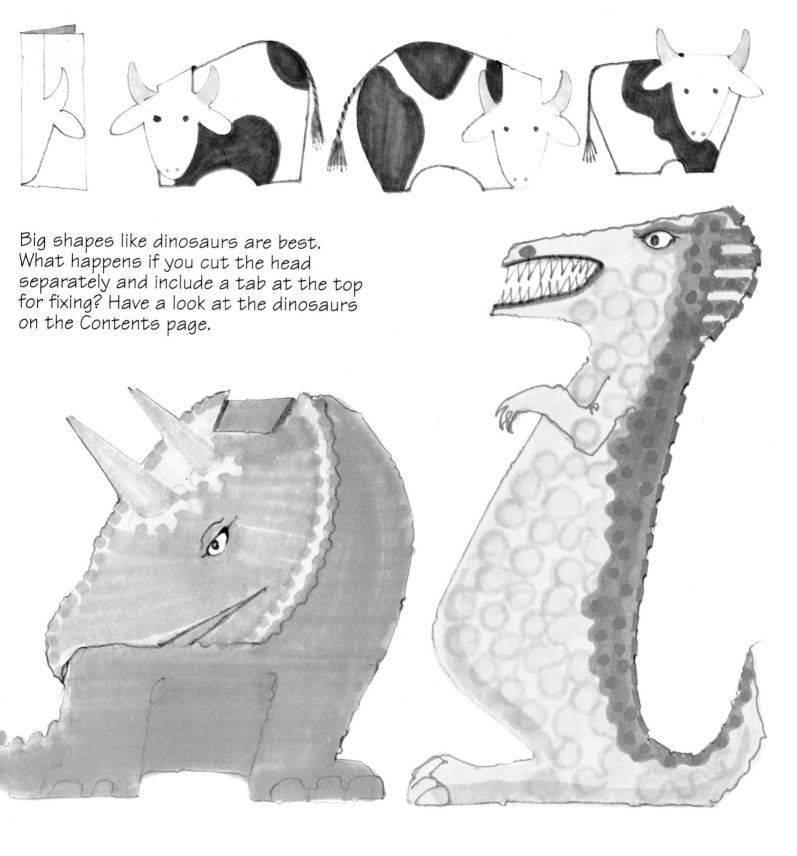

Big shapes like dinosaurs are best.
What happens if you cut the head
separately and include a tab at the top
for fixing? Have a look at the dinosaurs
on the Contents page.

Homes

If you have started to make models of people from different periods of history or from different places you might become interested in the way they lived, and the houses they lived in perhaps.

What shape were they? What materials did they use? You can make stand-up models of any sort of building — from a simple tepee to a multi-storey block. You might need pictures to work from, but try looking at buildings yourself when you go out, especially if you travel anywhere. You might be surprised at how different they are.

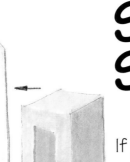

Surprise Street

If you begin to enjoy model making you can have fun making your own games. For SURPRISE STREET, you need to make a row of houses with front doors which open. The houses can be supported with a box at the back, with part of the box cut away at the front so that it becomes a small room behind the door. Once you have made the street you can decide what to put in the boxes – a letter with a message, a ghost, a sweet or candy, a growling dog or a lucky black cat. You can invite people when they arrive to choose one of the houses and open the door – they have only one choice. You can think of all sorts of surprises and have lots of fun.

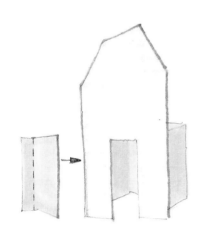

Boats

After starting to model people or buildings, you might go on to try some boats. At this stage you can begin to think of the way models can be built up by putting separate bits together. For a boat model, a simple hull shape can be supported with a box. How many bits would you need to put together to make this Viking ship? Just look closely at the illustration. You can do it.

1

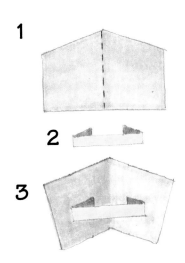

2

3

An interesting point about making simple boat models is that any boat is a good example of a symmetrical form – the same on both sides. Also, if you look at it from the front a single fold, like that on a greetings card, will help make the model stand. The fold can be secured at the back with a simple bracket, see pictures 1 to 3.

Using this technique – viewing the model from the front instead of the side – will let you make any boat, from an early sailing craft to something modern like a nuclear submarine or a hovercraft. Or a liner with tugs to tow it.

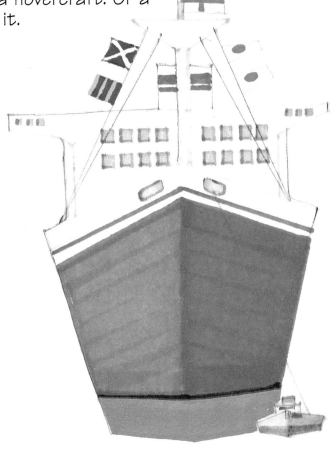

Hovercraft cut-out pattern

Pit Stop

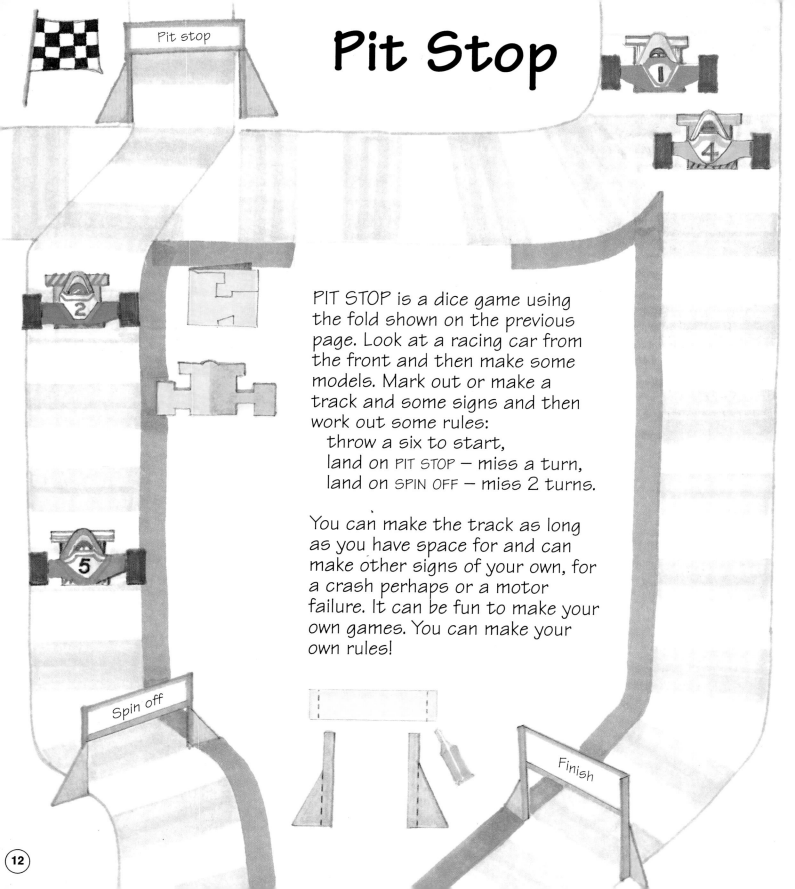

Pit stop

PIT STOP is a dice game using the fold shown on the previous page. Look at a racing car from the front and then make some models. Mark out or make a track and some signs and then work out some rules:

throw a six to start,
land on PIT STOP — miss a turn,
land on SPIN OFF — miss 2 turns.

You can make the track as long as you have space for and can make other signs of your own, for a crash perhaps or a motor failure. It can be fun to make your own games. You can make your own rules!

Spin off

Finish

Space Shuttle

If you use the centre fold in model making, you can also begin to add other simple features. Use the illustration as a pattern for a model of the American Space Shuttle. Trace the rocket and Orbiter shapes separately in paper and then cut them in carton card, each with a centre fold. Then make a tail for the Shuttle Orbiter, using the illustrated pattern which includes a sticking seam below the dotted line, see 1. Cut the tail shape twice, glue it together and add it to the Orbiter shape as shown in 2, 3 and 4. Decorate both shapes and stand or hang them for display.

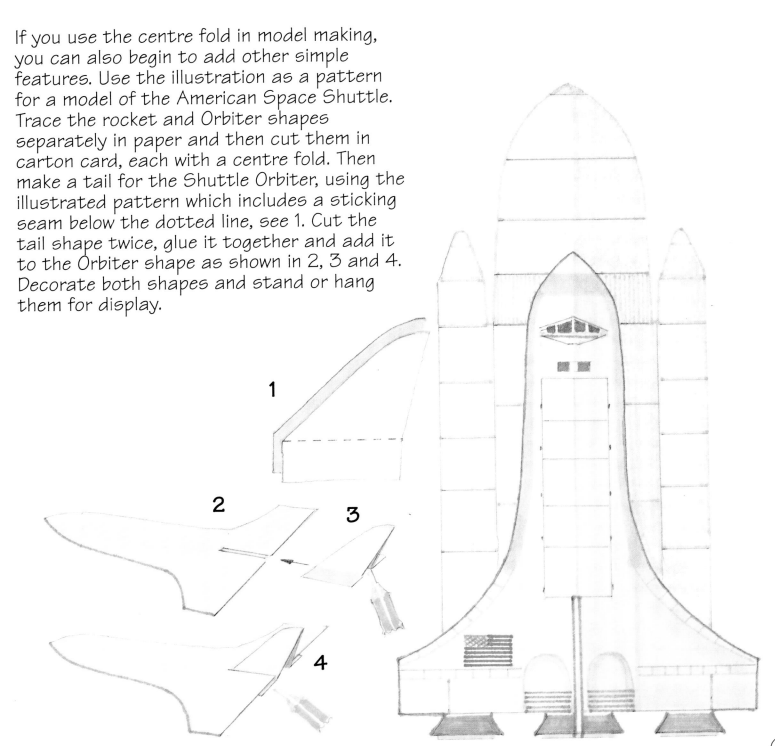

1

2

3

4

Dressed Figures

Using the centre fold again you can think about making standing figures with more modelled features. You can add simple hand shapes and ears, and you can use wool or string for hair. You might also want to cut clothes in paper or fabric, and can begin to shape the figures, taking care not to cut too much of the original shape away.

Arm

Hair

Hats

Legs

A simple shift is all you need as a pattern for clothes, and you can work in any period of history. Use your books. See how people used to dress, what sort of arms or armour they wore, and when you are modelling figures try making them in groups, especially if you want to display your work.

Cylinder Figures

You can make more figures by putting a simple cylinder head on a cylinder body. Just follow the illustrations, but be careful not to crush the head cylinder when you cut it.

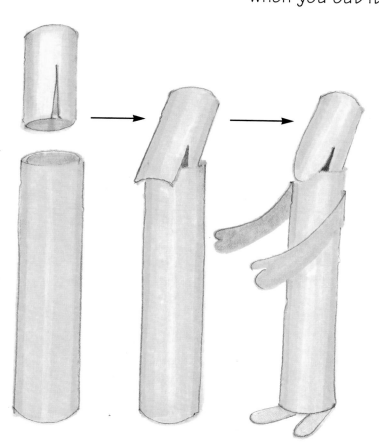

Seated Figures

If you add legs you can fold them so that the cylinder figure can be seated. Standing or seated cylinder figures can be decorated and dressed like any of the other figures you make.

Mounted Figures

1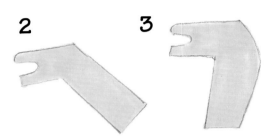

2 **3**

To make a horse cut a body shape in folded card, see 1, and another shape for the head and neck, see 2. You can vary the angle of the neck as shown in 3. Make a short cut into the fold of the body so that the neck can be inserted and fixed. If you cut two head shapes you can sandwich a wool or string mane between them. A folded figure can be dressed and set on the horse. Look at 4 and 5.

4

5

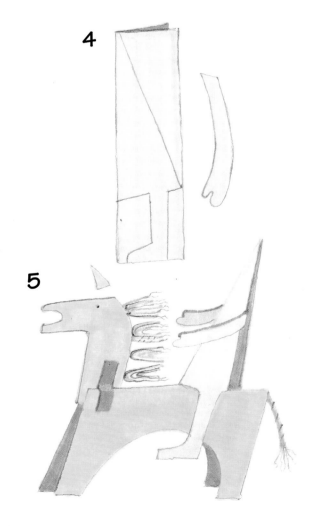

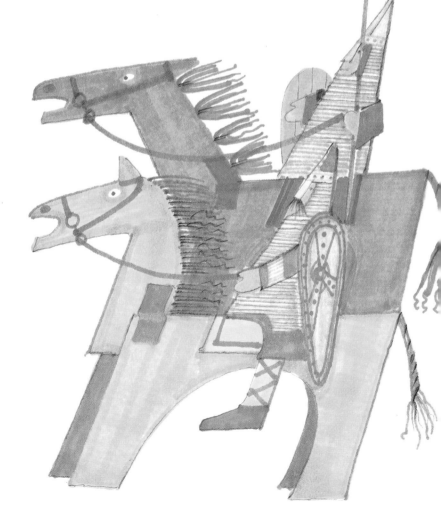

Cylinder Horses

Cylinder horses with cylinder figure riders should be easy now. You might have to do some snipping and trimming as you work, but this is usual in model making. The figure on the right helps you with the basics. Below are some suggestions for the finishing touches.

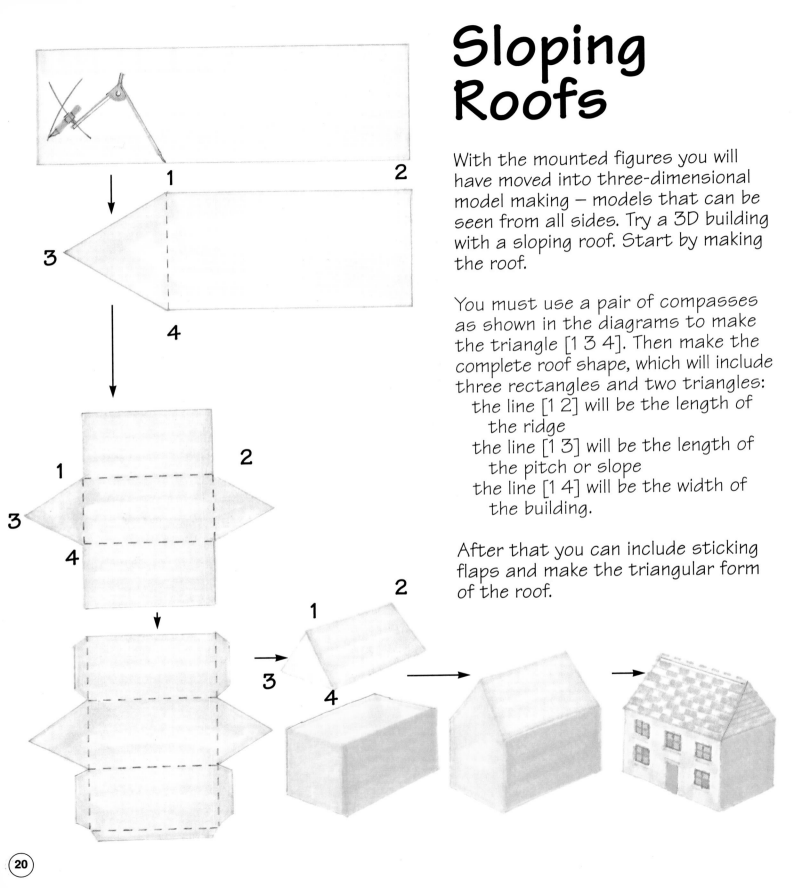

Sloping Roofs

With the mounted figures you will have moved into three-dimensional model making – models that can be seen from all sides. Try a 3D building with a sloping roof. Start by making the roof.

You must use a pair of compasses as shown in the diagrams to make the triangle [1 3 4]. Then make the complete roof shape, which will include three rectangles and two triangles:
   the line [1 2] will be the length of the ridge
   the line [1 3] will be the length of the pitch or slope
   the line [1 4] will be the width of the building.

After that you can include sticking flaps and make the triangular form of the roof.

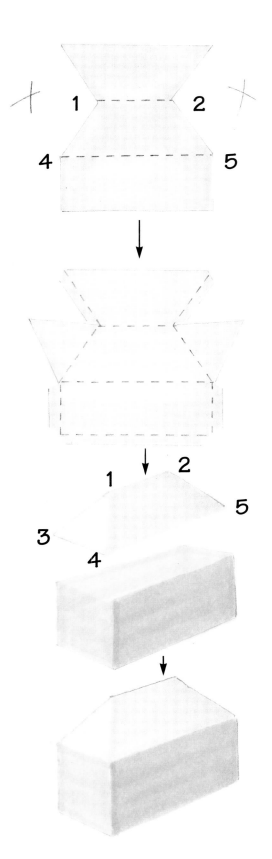

You will only use these two pages if you are modelling three-dimensional buildings. Remember — separate the roof from the building and plan it as a flat shape. Use a ruler to mark out the base of the roof as the lower rectangle and then use a pair of compasses as shown to find the triangles at each end.

A hipped roof (sloping in two directions) can be constructed in the same way.

A tower with a square pyramid on top is no more difficult. The square [6 7 8 9] must be started with the triangle [6 7 10] and three more triangles on an arc radius [10 7]. Not easy perhaps, but you can ask for help if you need it.

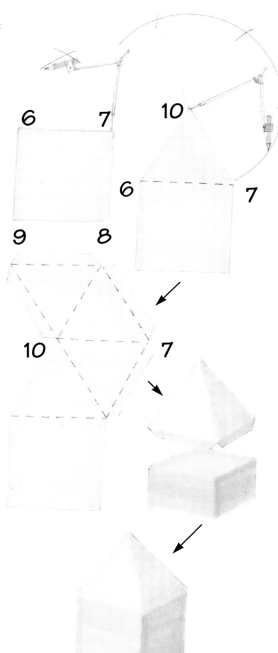

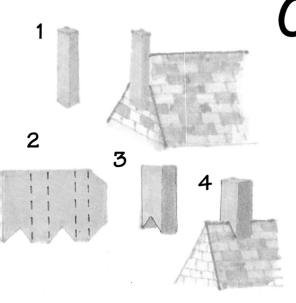

Chimneys, Doll's House and Shops

You can place a simple chimney form on the side of a building, as in 1, or cut it as shown in 2, 3 and 4 to sit on the ridge.

Cartons cut open on one side will allow you to construct a simple doll's house which you can have fun decorating and fitting with carton furniture. Or you can make your own row of shops. You can begin to use the skill you are developing as you work to make some toys, for yourself or perhaps for someone else.

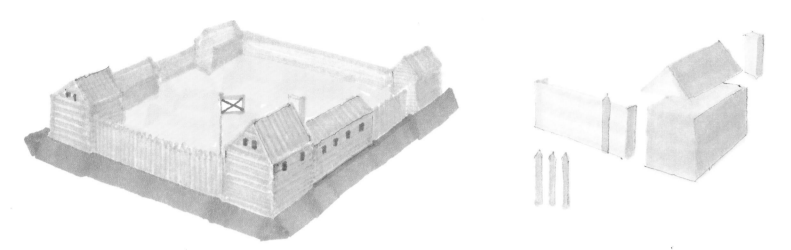

Any building project is possible if you see how it can be tackled by breaking it down into separate parts. It's exactly like building. You can model anything, from a frontier outpost to a fort.

When you have decided how to go about it, you can think about the finish you will give the model, and how you can imitate the material used in the original. Card shapes for stones can be cut and glued and pasted over with tissue. Anything which adds texture to a surface will help with a final effect.

Sailing Ships

From 3D buildings it is easy to move on to modelling 3D boats. On this page you can see how the Viking ship on page 10 can be tackled. You will need to work from picture references. It can be very interesting to research details you need for your models and you can enjoy learning as you work.

1

2

3

4

5

Mayflower

1

2

3

4

5

It is easy now to get into a jumbo jet and fly to America, but it wasn't always so easy. It was in the year 1620 that the *Mayflower* sailed from Plymouth in England with 102 men, women and children on board – less than the number who make Atlantic crossings daily in a jet. Making a model of the *Mayflower* should not be difficult for you now, and finding out what happened to the passengers and crew could be really interesting.

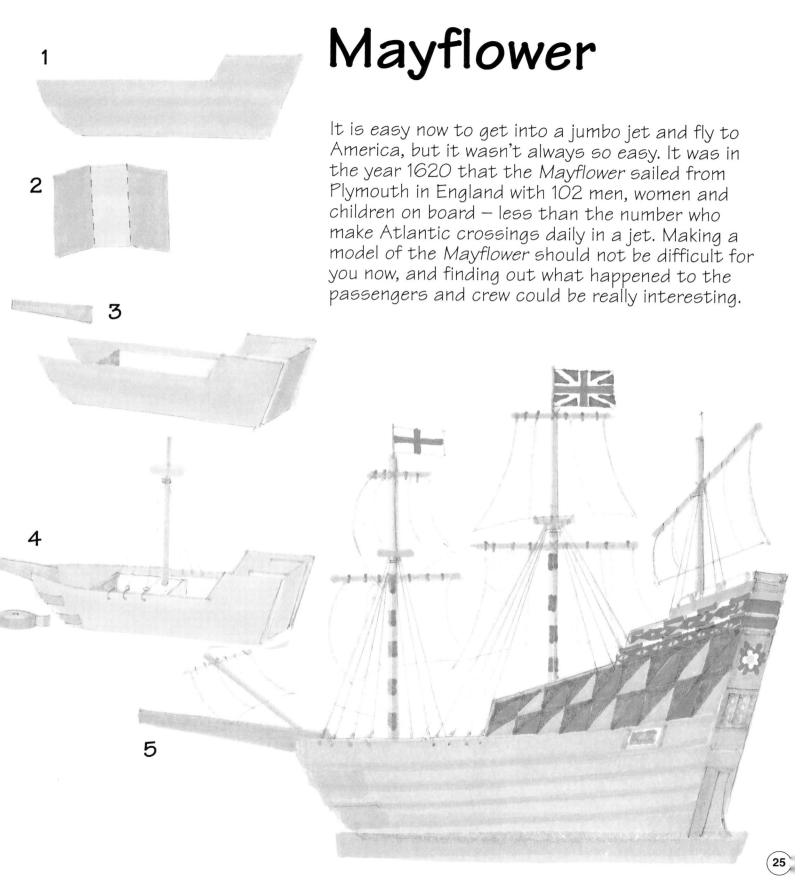

Container Ships

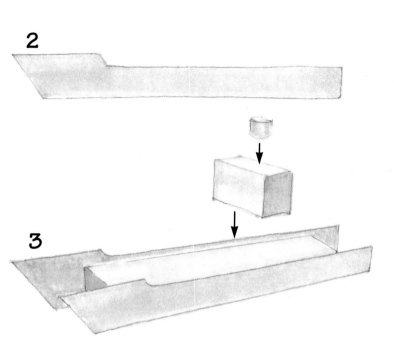

You can make your own Container Ship with a working crane for loading and unloading. Follow the pictures 1 to 4. Make a hook from a paper clip and cut and fix a cleat to the base of the crane, see 5 and 6, so that you can secure the lift-and-lower string! If you can make a round hole and insert the upright cylinder of the crane into the base, you will be able to swivel it from side to side as well as load and unload a cargo.

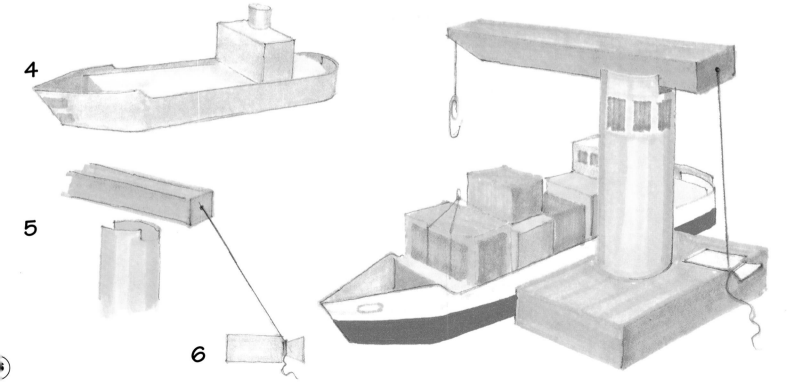

Roll-on Roll-off Ferry

Find two cereal packs and cut them to fit as shown in 1 and 2. Cut a bow shape in folded card, see 3, making sure it fits, and fix it with paper fasteners, see 4, so that it can be raised to allow toy cars on and off. You have a Roll-on Roll-off Ferry to play with. Of course real ferries are not as simple as this, but if you go to a travel agent and ask for a brochure you can make your model look very like the real thing.

1

2

3

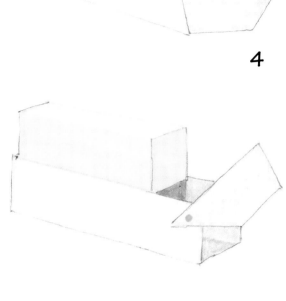

4

Wheels – Chariot Racer

1

2

3

4

Wheels can be a difficulty in model making, but for simple models a carefully cut circle of card can be fixed to an axle with a paper fastener. For the chariot you need the front and sides with sticking flaps, as in 1 and 2, to fold and fit to a base, see 3. Secure the wheels on to the base with paper fasteners, see 4. You have already seen how to make a standing figure and horse, and working from a good picture reference you should soon have your own Chariot Racer model.

Pioneering Waggon

If you have already made some Native American model figures, you can set them up with a model of the sort of travelling pioneers they might have met. Empty tubs cut to fit, or a curve of card, can be made for the waggon cover and this time instead of horses you will need to make longhorn cattle to pull the waggon. Just look closely at the pictures. The wheel spokes can be cut and added to the card discs to make them look more real.

Draw on spokes

Fix on wheels with paper fasteners

Pattern for cutout cattle

Tip-up Trucks

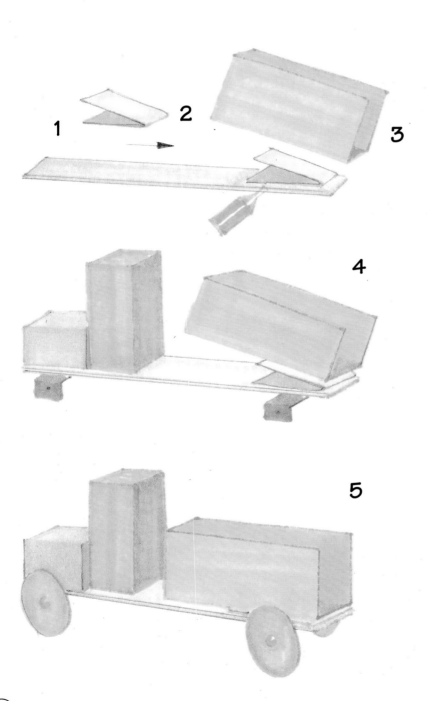

1

2

3

4

5

Start with a rectangle of card for a chassis, see 1. Make a folded card hinge, see 2, and cut a carton for the body, see 3. Stick them together as shown. Fix the hinged body to the chassis and add other cartons and wheels to complete the truck, as in 4 and 5. Decorate the truck with felt-tips and, where necessary, with paper you can draw on, putting in a driver for example.

Tankers & Articulated Trucks

Every day millions of empty cans are thrown away. It might be fun to make yourself a Tanker Truck with one of them.

For an Articulated Truck, you will need two strong card shapes for the chassis, see picture 1. You can join these with a paper clip and then develop the truck model, remembering that both parts will need double wheels on each side.

1

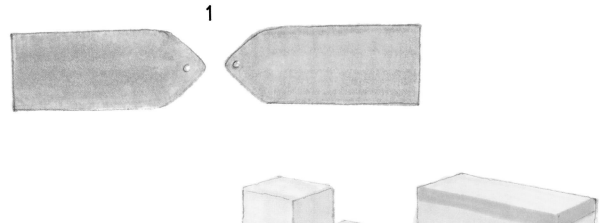

Going On

It is unlikely that many of us will have the opportunity to travel in space, but it could be fun to follow what the experts are doing. We could learn about what is happening as it happens or we could find out what has already happened in this wonderful time of space adventure. For example in May 1973, a Saturn V rocket was launched from the Kennedy Space Centre with Skylab, the first manned space station. If you were to save some of the rubbish thrown away every day, you could make a Skylab model and learn about things like the Apollo command and service module or about the solar array and the orbital workshop with its micrometeoroid shield.

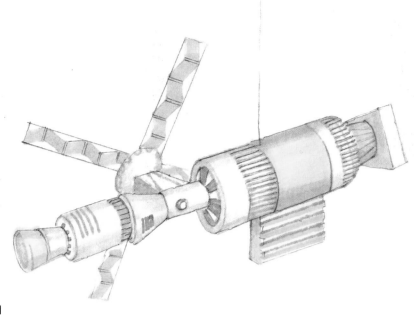

Making models can be fun. You can go back in history or forward into the future. You don't need a lot of skill. You need to know a little about what is possible and you need to be daring enough to experiment, asking yourself perhaps, 'How can I make that?'

You can do it! Just think how any model can be broken down into separate forms and shapes. and how you might be able to find these at no cost at all in scrap — odds and ends which are thrown away every day. Try it. Enjoy it — and see how much you can learn about so many things just by making fun models.